Mealtimes

Breakfast
Around the World

Gill Munton

WAYLAND

Mealtimes

Breakfast Around the World
Lunch Around the World
Evening Meals Around the World

Editor: Ruth Raudsepp
Designer: Joyce Chester

First published in 1998 by Wayland Publishers Limited,
61 Western Road, Hove, East Sussex, BN3 1JD, England.

© Copyright 1998 Wayland Publishers Limited

Find Wayland on the internet at http://www.wayland.co.uk

British Library Cataloguing in Publication Data
Munton, Gill
 Breakfast Around the World. – (Mealtimes)
 1. Breakfasts – Juvenile literature 2. Food habits –
 Juvenile literature
 I Title
 394.1'5

ISBN 0-7502-1973-4

Typeset by Joyce Chester
Printed in Italy by G. Canale & C.S.p.A., Turin

Picture acknowledgements

The publishers would like to thank the following for allowing their pictures to be reproduced in this book:

Axiom 22; Anthony Blake Photo Library 18; Bubbles/Loisjoy Thurston 29; Chapel Studios 17; Colorific! *cover* (bottom), 14; Eye Ubiquitous/Julia Waterlow 7 (bottom), 27; Chris Fairclough 10; FAO Photo Library 26; Farmers Weekly Picture Library 16; Ffotograph 4 bottom), 7 (top); Ole Steen Hansen *title page*, 8, 15; Hutchison Library 5 (top), 11, 25; Impact 13, 28; Christine Osborne 5 (bottom), 19, 24; Oxford Scientific Films *cover* (top); Peter Sanders 20; Still Pictures *contents*, 4 (top), 9, 12; The Travel Library 23 and Travel Ink/Angela Hampton 5 (middle), 6, 21.

Contents

Map of the world   4

Introduction   6

The big breakfast   8

Breakfast on the move   12

Beans, beans, beans!   16

Egg-stra special breakfasts   20

Do-it-yourself breakfasts   24

Breakfast in bed   28

Glossary   30

Books to read   31

Topic web   31

Index   32

Map of the world

In China, noodles are often served at mealtimes. There are many different kinds of noodle. They are eaten from a small bowl with chopsticks.

Wheat is an important crop in Morocco. In the villages, people use wheat flour to make their bread every morning.

All the countries marked on this map are covered in this book.

In the USA, many people eat a great deal of meat, dairy products and eggs. Fried eggs for breakfast are a special favourite.

CANADA

USA

COSTA RICA

Costa Rica is in Central America. Many Costa Ricans eat fresh fruit, such as watermelon and bananas, for their breakfast.

Some Aborigines still hunt animals for meat and gather fruit which grows wild in the bush. This is a bush orange.

Introduction

What do *you* like to eat for breakfast?

In this book you can find out about breakfast in lots of different countries. Some of the foods may surprise you.

Maria lives in Costa Rica.

Her breakfast is fresh fruit salad and a glass of orange juice.

Yasmin lives in Morocco with her family.

She is baking flat loaves for their breakfast in a special outdoor oven.

Dong, Xue and Xiaoli are eating breakfast in China.

They are eating deep-fried dough with vegetable soup.

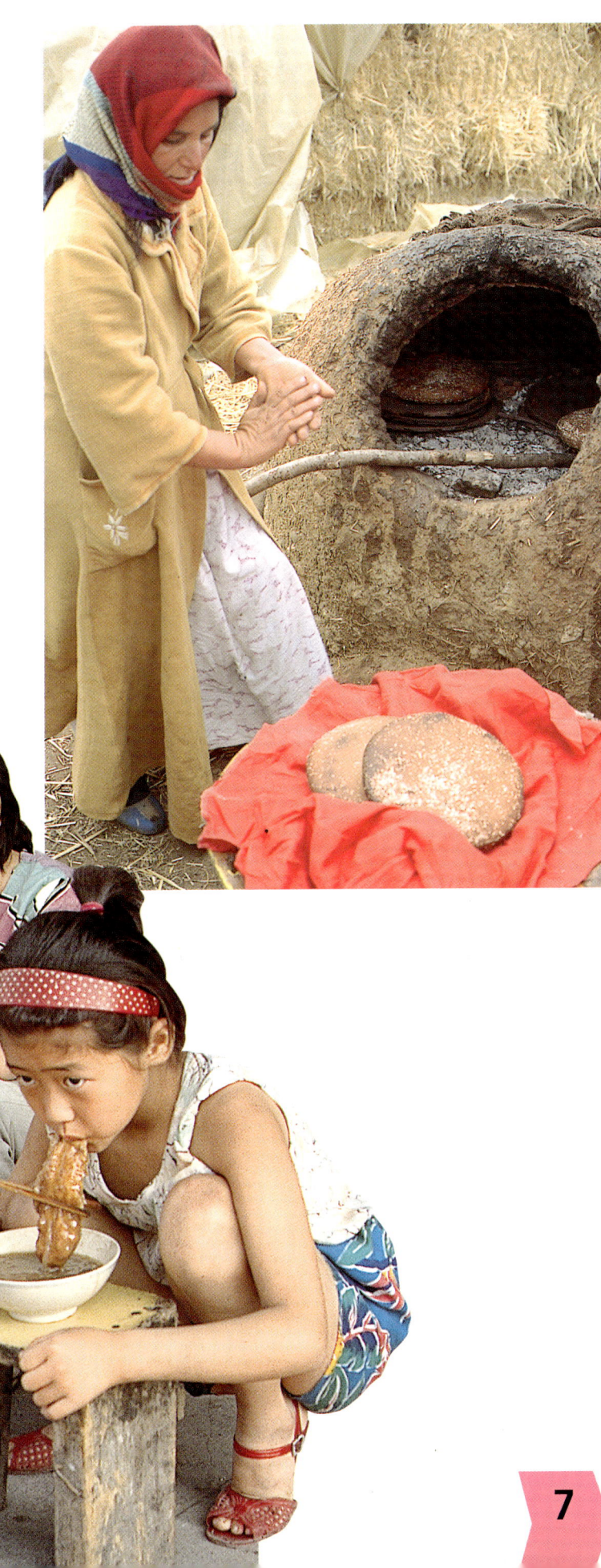

The big breakfast

This big breakfast comes from Denmark.

Farmers in Denmark keep large herds of cattle which produce milk, butter and cheese. All these foods are eaten for breakfast. People enjoy bread and cereals too.

Mai-Ling is enjoying her big bowl of noodles.

In China, even young children eat their food with **chopsticks**.

Alex eats a big bowl of porridge every morning.

He lives in the north of Scotland, where the winter weather is very cold. The porridge warms him up before he goes to school.

Sarah and Katie live in Florida in the USA.

This plate of fried eggs and pancakes is so big that they will have to share it. These eggs are called 'eggs fried sunny-side-up'.

Breakfast on the move

Linh lives in Vietnam.

She cycles to the bakery every morning to buy bread for her father's café.

Malik and his mother are going to eat breakfast on the train.

In Pakistan passengers have to buy food when they stop at a station. Malik's mother is buying **chapatis** from a food seller on the station platform.

Masako and her friends are eating noodles on their way to school.

Their snowsuits keep them warm in the cold Japanese winter while they eat their noodles on the roadside.

Steen and his father from Denmark are having breakfast up in the air.

Meals on an aircraft are served on small trays because there is not much room. Steen has everything he needs on his tray, even salt and pepper in tiny packets.

Beans, beans, beans!

Most baked beans come from the USA and Canada.

Baked beans begin their life as seeds inside the navy bean pod. The navy bean is a kind of **haricot bean**. This picture shows navy beans being harvested.

Everyone loves beans on toast.

Teresa lives in Ireland. She is having two helpings of beans on toast for breakfast because she is hungry.

These beans have been cooked with sausages and onions.

Beans cooked in this way are called Boston baked beans. Some Americans still cook Boston baked beans for supper on Saturday night and eat them cold for breakfast on Sunday morning.

Ali's father drives a donkey cart.

Ali and his father live in Pakistan. Ali is working with his father today, and they are sharing a dish of beans with the other drivers before they set off.

Egg-stra special breakfasts

Eggs are a favourite breakfast food in many countries.

Abdul and his son have a chicken farm in the Sudan. They collect the eggs every morning.

Scrambled eggs and black beans are a popular breakfast in Costa Rica.

This food is eaten by people who are going to go out to work all day.

Mai-Ling's grandparents sell eggs at the market.

They sell both boiled eggs and fresh eggs in this Chinese market. The boiled eggs have their shells dyed red to tell them apart from the fresh eggs.

Here are some Greek Easter eggs.

The eggs have been boiled and dyed red, and baked inside little bread rolls. This makes an egg-stra special breakfast for Easter morning.

Do-it-yourself breakfasts

Some people just pick their breakfast from a tree! This Australian fruit is called a bush orange.

Some **Aborigines** still live out in the **bush**. The men hunt and fish, and the women gather fruit, seeds, nuts and insects. The food they gather is called bush tucker.

Ronit is picking grapefruit for her breakfast.

She lives in Israel, on a **kibbutz**. Fruit and vegetables are grown on the kibbutz, and everyone helps to pick them.

The Pygmies of Central Africa gather their food, too.

Here two men are gathering honey. Some bees have made honey inside this tree-trunk, and one of the men is blowing smoke into a hole to make the bees come out. The other man is taking the **honeycombs** out.

Zoë lives in Athens in Greece.

On Saturday mornings she goes out with her friends. She buys her breakfast from a stall, and today she has chosen a bread ring.

Breakfast in bed

John is in hospital. He is getting better after an operation.

He eats his breakfast in bed, but soon he will be able to get up and eat his breakfast with the other children.

Babies have milk for breakfast.

William is only a few weeks old, and milk is all the food he needs for a few months. When he is about five months old, he will start to eat solid food.

Glossary

Aborigines The people who lived in Australia before the white *settlers* arrived.

bush Open, unfarmed land in Australia.

chapatis Thin rounds of bread, cooked on a hotplate.

chopsticks Thin sticks made of wood or plastic which are used instead of knives and forks in China, Japan and other countries in the Far East.

haricot beans Beans with light-coloured seeds that can be eaten. Some haricot beans are used to make baked beans.

honeycombs Waxy frames made by bees for storing their honey.

kibbutz A farm in Israel where several families live and work together.

Pygmies Tribes of hunter-gatherers who live in Central Africa.

settlers People who go to another country to set up their own community.

Books to read

Food series by Jillian Powell (Wayland 1996, 1997)

Food by Molly Perham and Julian Rowe (Mapworlds series, Watts, 1996)

Food Around the World series (Wayland, 1994)

What's Cooking? by Gabrielle Woolfitt (Wayland, 1994)

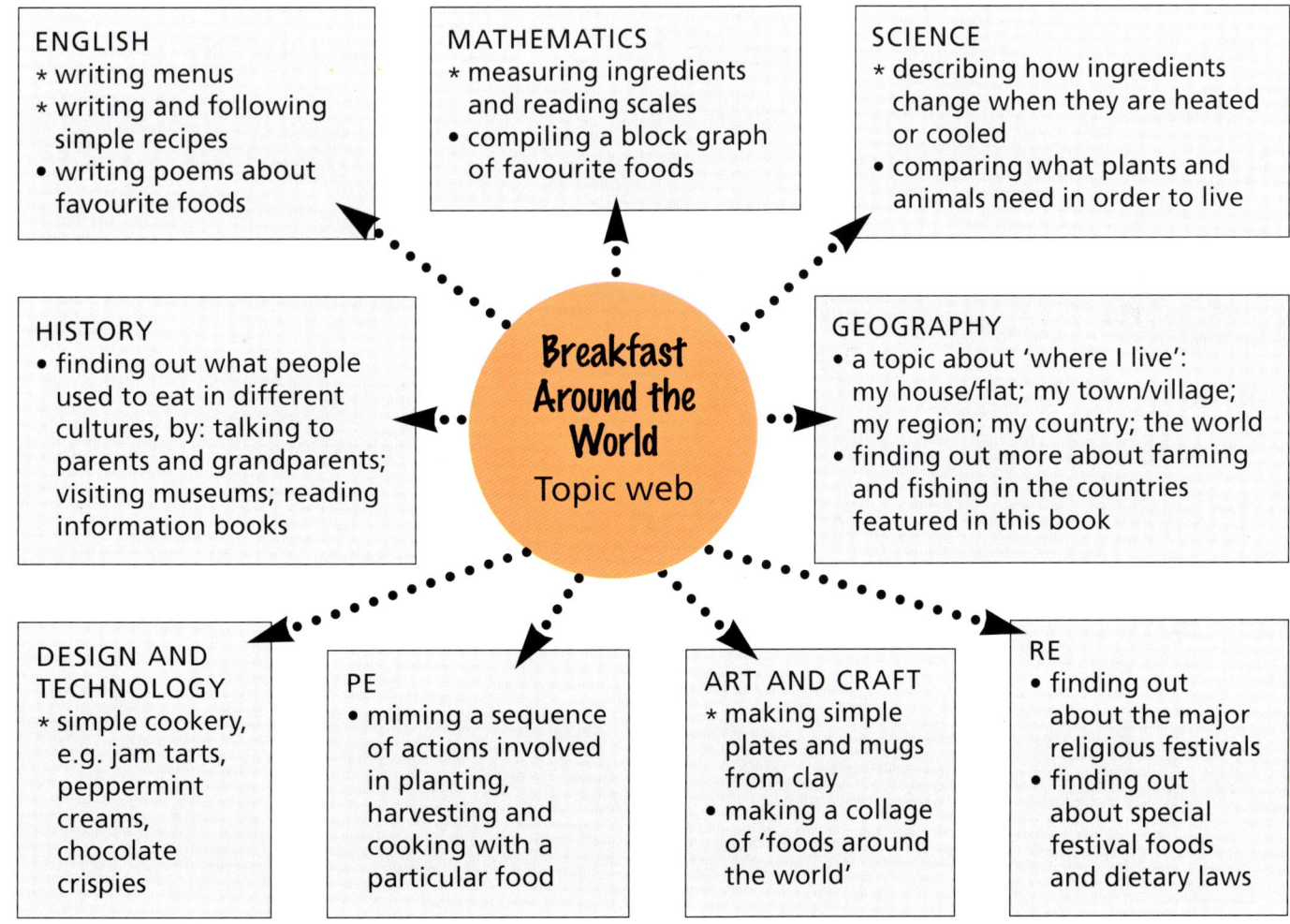

Breakfast Around the World Topic web

ENGLISH
* writing menus
* writing and following simple recipes
- writing poems about favourite foods

MATHEMATICS
* measuring ingredients and reading scales
- compiling a block graph of favourite foods

SCIENCE
* describing how ingredients change when they are heated or cooled
- comparing what plants and animals need in order to live

HISTORY
- finding out what people used to eat in different cultures, by: talking to parents and grandparents; visiting museums; reading information books

GEOGRAPHY
- a topic about 'where I live': my house/flat; my town/village; my region; my country; the world
- finding out more about farming and fishing in the countries featured in this book

DESIGN AND TECHNOLOGY
* simple cookery, e.g. jam tarts, peppermint creams, chocolate crispies

PE
- miming a sequence of actions involved in planting, harvesting and cooking with a particular food

ART AND CRAFT
* making simple plates and mugs from clay
- making a collage of 'foods around the world'

RE
- finding out about the major religious festivals
- finding out about special festival foods and dietary laws

* These could be linked to form a practical cookery project.

Index

Aborigines 5, 24
aircraft 15
Australia 5, 24

babies 29
beans 16, 17, 18, 19, 21
bread 4, 7, 8, 12, 27

Canada 16
Central Africa 26
cereals 8
chapatis 13
cheese 8
China 4, 7, 9, 22
chopsticks 4, 7, 9
Costa Rica 5, 6, 21

Denmark 8, 15

Easter 23

eggs 5, 11, 20, 21, 22, 23

fruit 5, 6, 25

grapefruit 25
Greece 23, 27

honey 26
hospital food 28

Ireland 17
Israel 25

Japan 14

kibbutz 25

milk 8, 29
Morocco 4, 7

noodles 4, 9, 14

oranges 5, 24
oven 7

Pakistan 13, 19
pancakes 11
porridge 10
Pygmies 26

Scotland 10
soup 7
Sudan 20

toast 17
train 13

USA 5, 11, 16, 18

Vietnam 12